THE SORE THROAT
& OTHER POEMS

by

AARON KUNIN

FENCE BOOKS
ALBANY, NEW YORK
2010

© 2010 Aaron Kunin
All rights reserved.

Published in the United Sates by
Fence Books
Science Library 320
University at Albany
1400 Washington Avenue
Albany, NY 12222

Book design by Mark Owens

Fence Books are distributed by
University Press of New England
www.upne.com

Fence Books are printed in Canada by
Westcan Printing Group
www.westcanpg.com

Libary of Congress Cataloging-in-Publication Data
Kunin, Aaron [1973–]
The Sore Throat & Other Poems /
Aaron Kunin
Library of Congress Control Number: 2010923755

ISBN: 978-1-934200-34-6

First Edition
10 9 8 7 6 5 4 3 2

For Lara Bovilsky

CONTENTS

Note on Method	ix
"You Won't Remember This"	1
A Word with You	9
"I Had You Here with a Wish . . ."	11
The Voice of the Earth	13
What's Your Pleasure, Brother?	14
A Can of Rats	20
Afterword	23
"The Age Demanded"	28
For Pleasure	35
[you say/you're sorry]	37
The Sore Throat	38
The Sore Throat	42
The Sore Throat	47
What Music!	50

The Sore Throat /or, This Machine Has No Body!	54
No Word, No Sign	58
The Sore Throat	62
The Sore Throat	63
Sore from Laughter	66
That Boy Is Thinking about the Word "No"	68
Your Money's No Good in Here	72
The Sore Throat	73
We Say No	75
[Disaster: he left a mess]	77
A Business Idea	78
God Is Not Cast Down	81
Asshole, Dickhead, Shit-for-brains	82
[king, you don't know, you don't]	83
What Other Eyes Do You Have for Me?	84
This Is about an Idea I Had Once, and I Think You'll Like It	86
[Music: "Why can't I be you"]	88

[more money, for a business, this is what]	89
[how/ can/ a/ word/ say/ it/ self]	90
The Sore Throat	92
[were you, to me, such a, would I]	97
[can see, in my, me a, say that you think]	98
[keep, where is, keep, that's]	99
[remember, music, how can I, idea]	100
The Sore Throat	101
Let My Brother Hear Music	102
It Is No Longer We Who Wish It	104
Knowledge Blobs	107

NOTE ON METHOD

The series beginning with "You Won't Remember This" is a translation of Ezra Pound's "Hugh Selwyn Mauberley" into a severely limited vocabulary of about 170 words. For Pound, "Mauberley" provided an occasion for disavowing his earlier work and for meditating on the uses of beauty for poetry. It was a way of asking the question: how could Pound write shallow poetry if he were not essentially a shallow person?

My translation is an inversion of Pound's psychological experiment. Instead of using "Mauberley" to go outside myself, to gain access to unfamiliar uses of language—which, for Pound, is the value of the poetic persona—I wanted to inhabit my personal 170-word vocabulary as fully as possible. Because I really believe that the part of yourself that you're most ashamed of is interesting and can be used as material for art.

The vocabulary derives from a nervous habit. For a long time, I have been compulsively transcribing everything I say, hear, read, or think—all the language I can pick up—into a kind of sign-language (technically a binary hand-alphabet) that looks more or less like fidgeting or piano playing. From the beginning, the compulsion did not focus exclusively on ambient language, because my hand continued to form words in the hand-alphabet even when there wasn't, apparently, anything for it to transcribe, at times when no one was saying anything and I wasn't reading or even thinking. At these times, my hand tended to repeat short phrases of indeterminate origin. For example: "It won't be easy and can't be a pleasure, it won't be easy and can't be a pleasure . . ." I kept a record of the phrases, and when the record included about 170 different words, I started writing poems with them, using the prosody, syntax, and thematics of "Mauberley" as a model. You could say that my project in these poems was to combine a rigorous formal procedure (writing within the limited vocabulary, and as much as possible—which is to say, not much—within the paraphrasable content of "Mauberley") with a kind of automatic writing (since the hand-alphabet represented, at least to me, a direct connection between my hand and my unconscious).

Many of the poems in the second series are called "The Sore Throat." These poems translate Maurice Maeterlinck's play *Pelléas et Mélisande* into the same limited vocabulary, now slightly expanded to include about 200 words. I don't know whether the poems could actually be staged. Maybe they narrate a performance of *Pelléas* for a community that only has 200 words at its disposal.

Maeterlinck's play is characterized by extravagant gestures. Perhaps the most famous scene is one in which Pelléas ties strands of Mélisande's hair to a tree and then climbs into the tree, thus creating, out of a projection from his lover's head, an environment that he can inhabit. What I respond to in the play, and in the musical adaptations by Debussy and Schoenberg, is the obsessive sensitivity to nuances of feeling. Pelléas and Mélisande are so timid, and their expressions are so precise, that they barely register on a human scale; whereas Golaud is a sort of raw emotion seeking to articulate itself. For me, Golaud is the interesting figure, because his problem— subjection to sensations for which he has no language— is also the problem of this translation.

Some of these poems first appeared in *Anomaly*, *Boston Review*, *The Canary*, *Fence*, *The Germ*, *No: A Journal of the Arts*, *Syllogism*, and *Titanic Operas*, and a few were reprinted in the anthologies *Isn't It Romantic: 100 Love Poems by Younger American Poets*, and *A Best of Fence: The First Nine Years*. An earlier version of *The Mauberley Series* is archived online at ubu.com.

"YOU WON'T REMEMBER THIS"

Last to know, and out of the mind,
You wish to begin the dance
Of pleasure; to heal "the soul"
And keep up the dance. Wrong from the start—

No, sorry, but you had been talking
About a brother you once had;
Moron; a change of mind;
And out of voice with easy change;

Just as you yourself must know
Sounded in the narrow throat;
Sobbing and weeping, vowing good habits,
You were like a machine of weeping.

Your Jesus, as it were, was fact:
Keep the mind on what you desire.
You say, "It may be I cannot"
And yet I like you as you are.

I do not know what is "like me";
By the machine of change
I let me down to wonder,
To suppose, to be demanded.

II.

The age demanded you-know-what
And what-have-you, a kind of
Weeping in laughter, and laughter
In weeping, not, anyhow,

The dance of the mind about the word,
Not (oh, brother)
Talking rats, the "moron,"—
No. That is not what we require.

At last the "age demanded" the laughter
Of a machine, applause,
A machine hard-on, not (my god!) a sigh
Or gasp left in the throat.

III.

Rats in the soul . . . and so on.

Rats in the bowels. Change yourself!

The voice was loud and hard,

The rats in your throat sounded great!

When I was a boy

I would see Jesus here.

"Say it with rats,"

As Jesus would have it.

I am of the earth;

What rats are you who remember

An age of wonder

When a kind of pleasure was possible?

So: begin. Begin: but how?

With my narrow mind, my sore throat,

I must seem right and good to you.

I damn myself and suppose myself a god.

A voice: "Here, have a can of earth."
"Um, that's all right."
By my habits you will know me,
By the habits I have on,

As the mind is, as it were,
A machine for knowing.
By the god! I know that you are right;
(But then, it contains rats).

Now, my brother can change into rats
At will. As for me, I can't complain.
How hard it is to change your habits.
Or not to have habits.

IV.

Anyhow, we do not complain
   And we do not heal, n'est-ce pas?

And vowing to have myself as you desire me,
my dear, for choice and for pleasure,
from habits of mind, after all
from good habits and bladder habits
for we know how to cope and when to weep
what with the way we keep weeping,
and how to cope with a fact of mind;

For us, the sore will not heal
   "it won't be easy and can't be a pleasure"
and a machine contains us
that can no longer keep in mind
from the mean of the mind, to keep
me from mind, and up to the throat
(that is, to mind myself, do you mean?);
the word is "keep out"

And it seems to change.
Eyes of the soul and eyes of the mind,
last laughter and the last dance,

at last, a word with you

at last a word with the machine
I'll have a word for every fact
(but you must remember all of it)
then, at last, the laughter of a moron.

v.

We know what choice we have,
And what is up to us:
We do not complain for a can of rats.
But there's no way left

For the great voice to keep talking,
And easy eyes are no good for seeing

But for weeping for the good that we remember,
For the dance of hard fact upon our dear earth.

A WORD WITH YOU

But you can't keep me here.
I wonder what it is to be just.
Or is it impossible?
Ah, it must be possible, otherwise

We would not have a word for it.
The word is a fact, after all;
We can be sure of that,
Just as our talking is a kind of fact.

The eyes, the voice, the fact
Of your narrow throat, ah!
Remember that your talking habits
Change the word, and change who you are.

And so I say to you now
That all our fact is no more than a guess:
For a word contains the guess,
Like a sigh sounded within laughter,

And your voice will keep on talking
When the fact of it is no more.
The machine seems to have eyes.
But what can it know?

For the machine must have our habits.
My god! How the machine can gasp,
Sob, sigh, and weep.
And yet, it is not like us.

"I HAD YOU HERE WITH A WISH..."

I had you here with a wish
On a "suppose"; to start with me.
Now hear a wonder—
Hear me! Oh, I would you would!

I like you. I like the machine.
When I was a boy, the rats were longer
And, it seems, would always be talking...
But what was it the rats demanded?

"A machine for you": yes,
That is it. Now I remember.
Machine, heal yourself! A wonder:
Why am I talking to a machine?

I like the machine: why?
"Remember me always," as Jesus would say;
How will the machine remember us
When we have left it? And then,

Rats are like you.
But that boy is more like you.
The way is narrow and hard
And our habits are not easy with us.

THE VOICE OF THE EARTH

"Sigh" is a word
For a kind of sobbing;
"Sobbing": that is
A kind of weeping;

A whine, a gasp, a sort of a sigh:
That is "talking"—
Out of the throat
Cast.

WHAT'S YOUR PLEASURE, BROTHER?

Now, what I like is the right word.
My soul seems easy when I have it right;
Otherwise, there's no pleasure on earth
    Can keep me easy.

Or suppose you had the mind of a moron.
For the moron, what's good is a hard-on
Always hard: longer, wide, and always easy,
And weeping, weeping with pleasure
And laughter. Yeah, he would like that;

Had you been a moron, you would wish for it.
But you desire much more than this,
More than pleasure, more than talking,
More than a dance with this boy or that boy,

But what you desire is not on the earth.
As for the rats: the rats "demanded a change"
To start with; and the right to say
What you know in your mind; the right

To easy talking; the right to complain
About the moron; then, choice for all rats,
And no more goddamn can.

A moron can be right. It's possible.
Maybe he is, maybe you are.
To be right is possible. But is it easy?
Talking is easy. To be god is easy.

x.

What's good for god is good for you
And me, and, in fact, for all of us,
For god is all-in-all; so all that is
Is more good than you know.

And so it seems that god can do no wrong
And that's all to the good, and it is a pleasure;
It is a pleasure and impossible,
For the way of right is narrow and hard,

And the wrong way is wide and easy
On the eyes, and the mean is hard to keep to.
Now hear the word of god: "It's not that there's
No right-and-wrong here; there's no right."

XI.

I am my talking habits,

So I am a cast of mind;

I must complain,

And yet my habits are a pleasure to me.

But I do not suppose

That pleasure is "the possible."

The wonder of it is,

That rats can keep it up without a bladder.

XII.

"You are like a god to me; for me
The good is you." N'est-ce pas?
You are dear to all who know you
And to me. You are all my good.

Seeing you there with your throat
And your eyes, all in down habits;
Eyes that I myself would wish for,
Eyes that are narrow, like rats's-eyes;

Seeing into your eyes, and, ah!
Down your throat; and your voice,
How it seems to dance with laughter;
And your wide soul, that contains

All pleasure and goodness; I gasp;
I am just a boy or moron;
Now, after the dance, seeing as your eyes
Are upon me, what can I do

But wish that it may always be so?
Or would you have my eyes to weep always?
I know you're not here.
And I seem to hear your voice . . .

You mean so much to me—just to hear
You talking with a vowel in your throat!
I like you more than I can say;
There is no word can mean so much!

I'm sorry for that. I have sounded
The bowels of all my talking:
It sounded great; it's no longer possible.
You are a word.

A CAN OF RATS

Begin—can you cope—

    "Oh, say can you see"—laughter—

Applause—can you cope—

    I know—before you were, I am—after

You are, I am—but what I am—I don't know—

    Your eyes are the machine of all my woe—

I wonder—can you cope?

Earth—keep up the dance—

       And yet—I can no more—

Mind—keep up the dance—

       But as for me—therefore

I cannot—I am not he—

       You know it's not so easy

As that—keep up the dance.

Dear—as you desire me—

      So let me seem—I change all my good

To weeping—with a word—

      But for me—all would be right

And good—there would be

      No wrong on earth—but for me—

As you desire me—so let me appear.

AFTERWORD

Pleasure is but a can
Of earth, and the soul
No more than
A great bladder.

A can of Jesus is our god,
A can of Jesus and/or rats;
The rats are weeping;
Jesus is the earth;

The earth is your brother.
Here are your good habits.
Say it
In a voice so loud,

So loud that Jesus can hear it,
So loud that I can no longer hear it.
That voice! You sounded
Just like my brother.

XV.

"But how can the machine know what the soul is, and how can it begin to remember?

"As the machine cannot dance, as the machine cannot hear the voice or see the word, how can it begin to suppose that there is a pleasure in the mind yet more dear? And that all other pleasure is just a great sore, and not to be demanded?"

Out of the mind once more, my soul;
As you were talking to yourself,
All will narrow
To a word within, at last, a word.

A word within a word, weeping
For a word, and sounded then
Like rats in the eyes of desire.

A word . . . a word that will last
Longer, and cast about as I can.
The machine let out a whine,
"Keep it to yourself" . . .

Oh to be a machine . . . to say
A word, and not to mean
By it. Then, to mean all . . .
As a boy may have

A change of mind;
And the earth contains you.
And god contains the earth.
A machine contains that—

Maybe there is no word for it—
All-knowing, all-seeing:
A machine, therefore.
May I say another word about it:

The will to change,
Into a god!—

To change one word into you-know-what.
To change the soul into a machine
Of yourself, and rats into rats
Of the mind. The will to remember:

Out of desire, a word is sounded,
For it is the will of god,
All-knowing, all-seeing, and so on.
—Remember who was good and kind to you

When god would not let you have
So much as a damn.
—Right.
But don't.

"THE AGE DEMANDED"

You are like us. Or you are not.
Anyway, you are not
What we require, you are not,
Ahem, what we demanded,

That's for sure. You are like us:
What you have to say, we know.
We say it always. As you begin to say
It, there it is. We say it now.

It is in the throat now
And we are talking about it
As always. We know all that we know
By, of, for, within, and out of it.

For talking habits are habits
Of the mind, as you know.
The word, as it were, is our god:
We cannot change it, we have no choice.

        You are not like us; what you have
        To say, we cannot begin
        To know. We cannot hear it.
        Or suppose we hear it (we do not):

What can it mean? Out of your throat
You have sounded a hard word, a word
Impossible. What word it is
We do not know: we do not

Remember it; we cannot
Keep it in the mind; it seems
Longer to us than it is, maybe,
Like a word sounded down in the bowel.

But we can complain about it.
Maybe we can change it.
So let's have it.
You must say it now, my dear;

Otherwise, how will we know?
Rats to you, and up your bowel;
Keep it in your bowel, rats to god;
Hear me with eyes, can you?

Rats in a can, oh boy!
But what-for and why-why?
Here's to you, brother, and here's to you;
Here's to the word of god and your brother;

Here's to all the pleasure we can't have;
Here's to the boy that your god had, Jesus;
Here's to the sore that Jesus had
That will not heal and is a wish;
Here's to the habits you cast out; here's to

The habits you keep, and the habits of god.
Here's to rats! What rats? There are rats:
Down on the earth. Out, rats; damn you!
Let me have rats, rats for a change!

As for you—no more, I say,
No more, with all my soul.
Every Good Boy Demanded Fact . . .
How much longer can you keep it up?

This is not what I had in mind:

How much longer do I have to be in it?

It's impossible. But I have

A machine to do it for me. Dear machine—

You are not so much a brother

To me, more of a god, I guess.

I am in the right. My laughter is the last.

That boy had a mind like a machine.

XVII.

I have a voice, but no throat;
I am a word all vowel;
I have no eyes, but I am all-seeing;
I am but a boy, and my age is great;
Now I am in your bladder.

Who am I?
The machine is sorry for me,
I know, and what a pleasure
It is. Now you know why I require

A machine: for pleasure.
I have a soul: as for the machine . . .
You are right, I am
The machine: a good guess.

You must be a god: yeah, right.
What kind of god is that? Can you
Change woe and weeping to pleasure
And loud laughter? Then do it.

You must be the god of weeping.
But you keep talking.
A good god for us
In the age of the weeping moron.

Say otherwise:
"And now I cannot wonder.
So I must whine;
No change."

FOR PLEASURE

"Sigh no more," moron, sigh no more!
Let laughter have voice, for a change;
Let there be pleasure, let there be goodness;
Be kind, be kind and be knowing!

Let like keep with like, and no more
Weeping; let rats dance with rats and
Not be sorry; let laughter last
Longer than weeping.

And Jesus will appear to sort out
The good rats from the rats
That are left, and the god
Will say with loud voice: "Be rats!

And I will be hard with you, for all
That you complain: may the earth
Be sore with you upon it;
May the earth always be in your way."

you say   but you're

you're sorry   not sorry

THE SORE THROAT

Last to know, and out of the mind, always.
Just as you yourself must know, n'est-ce pas?
Out of the mind, and wrong from the start.

Here is the earth, and you are on it. The earth is great: it's wide and narrow and easy and hard. Here is a throat for you to keep: it contains a voice. I am here: I am a good boy, I am a good moron. What you demanded from the earth, you now have, and there is a god. I wonder why you are weeping.

I no longer wish to remember
Seeing you gasp with laughter.

Here is the earth: what's on it nowadays, I wonder? It's a pleasure to be on the earth in the age of talking rats. What's wrong with you is that you always complain about the loud moron.

    A change in the habits of rats —
    Rats of the mind, that is.

Is there a moron? But how would you desire to say it? You have a choice. It's for your throat. Your talking habits are no good. I will always sigh for myself, for I know that I am the moron. I am sure of it.

    It is hard to hear the voice of god;
    It seems so narrow now.
    But the last of the rats
    Will remember it with pleasure.

Now the talking will begin. Jesus will do the talking, and the rats will do the weeping. But hear the voice of the moron: "The eyes of god are upon you." How much longer will the moron be talking, can you guess?

And you know—you are dear to all rats. The god of the rats would say: "Don't be sorry. For pleasure is in the mind, and it is a god." How great is the goodness of the god of the rats—how good, how wise and kind! But remember the narrow way of Jesus: "Dance and be easy with yourself, but god will damn you for it."

>Oh boy, oh brother, oh dear, my dear
>It won't be easy and can't be a pleasure.

Always begin weeping: the rats are weeping. Begin in wonder: the rats are weeping and sobbing. But there will be good habits and so on: the rats will be longer. The rats demanded a change. But the rats will always say: "We have no choice." Jesus cannot remember why; Jesus is wrong.

> I have to know about the dance
> Of the good rats.

You are good for seeing and pleasure; your good habits are talking and laughter. I wonder why you are weeping with your brother, the moron.

THE SORE THROAT

The throat is
sore for a
word. It is
sore with word-

desire, desire
for the word "she."
The word "she": will
it appear? Will

she appear?
(Is the word
"she" a she?)
She is a

word I always,
without knowing,
had in my mind.
Once, to my shame,

I had no
idea
what to do
with the word

"she"; now it seems
like I don't know
any other
word. It seems like

everything
is a she,
money is
a she (you're

so complete you
don't have to think
about money!
You have so much

money you
don't know what
knowing is!),
knowing is

a she, and in
heaven, god is
a she. No more
Herr Gott, from now

on, no more
seigneur, no
more boy-god:
the end! But

won't she start to
wonder: "If there's
no word for 'he,'
if everything

is a she,
why would we
have to have
a word for

it? If this word
appears every-
where, it won't mean
anything." And

at last she
may say to
you: "You are
my own good

boy. For me
there's no choice:
no other
boy will do."

THE SORE THROAT

I can't seem to say anything more. There's
something wrong with my throat.

                     — Our purpose is,
concealing the mess and the rats; otherwise,
the seigneur will complain that there are rats
everywhere.

            There's a word in my throat!

— Can't you let it out with your voice?

                         Not possible.
The word is too wide, my throat too narrow;
there's something in the way.

—I can hear it:
the word "she."

How can you hear it if it's
in my throat?

—I doubt that you can hear it.

Ahem.

—Was that a complete word?

No. There's
more of it left in my throat.

—Out of the way.

—The seigneur is on his way.

—He will be
here any day now.

—You must let us out
now.

—We have so much to do.

I wish I
had a machine that would say what to do.

— I'll begin by concealing this mess. There
must be a hundred thousand rats out here.

Two hundred thousand. It's impossible.

WHAT MUSIC!

Here is what he seems to say: "Dear brother,
there has been a change. Remember the money
I left with you, so that you would have something

to start a business? I now require it
for another purpose. The purpose is
music"—he seems to like music more than

money—"You don't know a thing about music,
what it can do to the body, the mind,
and so on. You don't know what it means

to desire music. You don't know how it
can mess with you down there. Your dick in my ass,
music, and I don't like it, but I desire it.

Your dick in my throat, and talking is difficult.
Your dick in my throat, oh collusion, and
it's not what I desire, but it will keep

me hard. I throat your hard-on, seigneur, and
it's horrible to me, but nothing can
keep me away from it. You shit on me,

music, and at last my pleasure and shame
are complete, and I don't wish to have it
end. At last I'm sore down there, and I must

have it again. Change money for music,
brother, and weep. And yet it has beauty—
when I hear it, the voice that she has

has such beauty, I can no longer
remember anything else. And yet
there is shame in it"—yes, there is shame—

"or there may be a kind of shame in my
impossible desire for the money.
May I have it?" What do you say to that?

—I say nothing. I have nothing to say.
Remember my age: and yet I know nothing
about myself. What can I know about
another? Think about it: what do I
desire if not to do good? If not the
good? . . . But I wonder, what good is it to
do what I do? What good is it to have
a body? To have a voice if nobody
can hear it? To have a mind that only
seems to doubt all that it would like to think?

To have a soul without knowing god? And
to have eyes? My eyes are bad, they are "good
for weeping but not for seeing," and eyes
not good for seeing are good for nothing.
But what good is seeing, what is seeing
for? Seeing is just another way of
concealing what is there. The purpose of
the eyes, the purpose of the body, is
to keep the mind from knowing anything.

THE SORE THROAT
OR, THIS MACHINE HAS NO BODY!

The throat is sore for a word. It is sore
with word-desire, desire for the word "I."

—I am not a word. "I" is an other!

I myself am a word.

      —Sorry, "I myself"
is more than a word.

      Not if you say it
like this: "Imyself." Or like this:

I I I I I I IIIII I   IIIII
II II II I I   I   I
I I I I   I IIII I   III
I   I I   I I   I   I
I   I I II   IIIII IIIII I

—Let me say it for you. I'll say it without a word:

"The throat is sore for a word. It is sore
with word-desire, desire for the word 'you.'
It would like to say: 'My eyes are sore
from seeing you, just as my mind is sore
from the idea of you. I wish I had
no eyes: without eyes I wouldn't be seeing
you so much. Without eyes there would be
no seeing. I wish I had no voice: without
a voice there would be no talking—that way
it wouldn't be possible for you to hear me.

I wish I had no throat: no throat, no voice,
right? And it wouldn't always be sore—sore
from talking and sore from not talking, sore
for a word I wish to say, but don't. So,
at last, without my throat, the soreness would
be nowhere, by itself, its own thing, and not
in me. I wish I had no body: if
I had no body, how would you know that I
was there? You would not. I would not
disgust you anymore. Without a body
and without desire, I would have no start
and no end, and it would be heaven. I wish
I had no mind, so I wouldn't have to think
about you (what would it be like to be
a moron and have no mind? I would say
to every idea, every doubt, every toy
of the mind: away with you!). I wish I
had no soul, and god would not own anything

in me. God would have no business with me.
Nothing would keep me on earth or in heaven
or anywhere else. No body, no mind,
no soul, no throat, no voice, no eyes: what's left?
What else can I disown? No "I." No self.'"

NO WORD, NO SIGN

There's no word for you. There's no word
for what you do to me. For what you do,
somehow, and you don't know you do it,
to my mind with just your voice, so that

everything I once was sure of seems wrong;
for what you do to my way of seeing,
so that I start to doubt my own eyes if
what my eyes report isn't just like what

I hear you say; and for what you do to
my voice to keep it from talking, to keep down
every word somewhere where I can't remember
it: for this, there's no word. To me

you're like a machine without a purpose,
whose purpose is to cast doubt on every
idea that my mind is thinking, and
the end of every idea is you.

You, to me, are a kind of fault in the
mind, a complete system of bad habits,
a video that I keep seeing or a word
I keep saying (do I have a choice?), and

this word has no meaning, and anyway
it's not a word, for there's no
word that contains what you are. You are
what the rats were talking about when they

demanded the "thing-in-itself." You are
nothing like what I had in mind, nothing
less than a complete disaster for my
word-system. You are the body whose voice

I seem to hear saying: "You must change your
habits" (if you change your habits what's left
of you? How will you know who you are? For
you're nothing if you change your way of seeing

and thinking: where the word "you" appears I
seem to mean "myself"). For I change when I'm
with you. This is something you can't know. But
I'm sure you won't doubt me if I say: "Seeing

you I change into something else (a change
for the good? Maybe I like myself more
when I think that you like me—I know you
don't, but I don't always remember)." Always

remember: there is no you. Remember,
when I say the word "you," I'm not talking
to anybody. When I say "you" I'm
inventing you (for what?). I'm inventing

a word for a thing that isn't there. "Your
brilliant eyes" (I'm inventing the eyes); "the
end of your dick" (inventing it); "the sound
of your voice" (a sound in the mind, a sound

I won't ever hear anywhere else). When I
see you, I'm seeing an idea of you.
You are a wish for there to be somebody
who will hear my voice. You are my wish for

there to be another body. You are
a choice my mind seems to desire naturally,
as a word would desire a thing. A choice
is a thing (you're my choice). But I'm nothing.

THE SORE THROAT

Laughter is a way of knowing
or a sign of knowing, a way
of saying that you know something

without saying what it is (you
think you know but it's not what you
think) about. Is it possible

that when I was talking about
laughter, I was, in fact, thinking
about — something else?

THE SORE THROAT

I'm inventing a machine
for concealing my desire.
And I'm inventing another
machine for concealing the
machine. It's a two-machine
system, and it sounded like
laughter. And I'm inventing
a machine for concealing
the sound. You, to me: "Why are
you concealing the beauty
of your machine?" Every machine
has more beauty than the last,
for everything whose purpose
is to conceal seems to change,
in the end, into a sign
of what it's concealing. And

now the sound that once sounded
like laughter is so loud that
it seems more like sobbing or
laughter concealing sobbing.
All my inventing is a
complete disaster. It's not
concealing my desire, it's
talking about my desire
to conceal my desire, like
a voice on a message machine
that would say: "Hello. About
desire, I'd like to say a
word or two. It's not your eyes,
it's not the word you say, it's
not your complaining voice that
I desire. All I desire
is your applause." It's hard not
to hear what the message is

saying, also it's hard to
keep myself from inventing
another machine to keep
from hearing it. So invent
a machine for disinventing.
This will be the last machine
I ever invent, and its
purpose will just be to change
every machine into shit.
No more inventing (for me).

— What a shame. It once was a
wonder of a machine; now
it's more like a disaster.

— I think he left a message …

— You're wrong: he just left a mess.

SORE FROM LAUGHTER

The eyes that you have,
how like the eyes of
a boy they are!

        —Maybe
I'm from heaven?

        Can
we have such eyes?

        —I
don't know what you mean
by "eyes."

What word do you have

for eyes? A can of

eyes?

    —Change can to can't.

THAT BOY IS THINKING ABOUT THE WORD "NO"

Your eyes say no.
Your voice seems to
say no.

    —You're just
like the other
who was here.

        Who
was here?

    —I won't
say! I won't say!

No more weeping,

don't be crazy,

I'm not concealing

anything, I

was just talking,

just talking . . .

What's that down there?

—Oh! That is the

toy he left me.

Would you like your

toy? Here, let me . . .

There's nothing wrong

with it, I don't

think, or if there

is . . .

— No, no I
don't wish to have
it.

I'll heal it
for you, it will
be a pleasure
to do this for
you.

— You can keep
it! I don't wish
to have it! I
would say to that
toy: to hell with
you! I will keep
to myself. I
will not hear what
you have to say.

You don't like your
toy? All right—but
it would be an
easy thing to
heal it. And it
appears to be
an otherwise
good toy.

YOUR MONEY'S NO GOOD IN HERE

That's not the kind I like. Don't you have the kind I like?

—Why don't you just say what kind you like, dear. Or else I'll have to guess.

You always have to guess. And you always guess wrong. And when you say your guess, I change.

THE SORE THROAT

I guess I'm with you.
But I don't know where
I am.

    —Don't know where
I'm from.

        I don't know
where you're from myself.
Do you remember
your age?

        —Maybe a
hundred. Or maybe
less.

I was concealing
some money, about
two hundred thousand
dollars, but I don't
remember where I
left it.

—Maybe you
were concealing it
from yourself?

This is
no place for you to
be by yourself.

—Oh!
Do not do anything
to my body!

WE SAY NO

We say that this

or that "is" or that it "seems." We say that
this or that is or seems "good" or "bad," that
that thing that we require so that BODY
will last; so that MIND will think what is right,

guess what is wrong, doubt the impossible;
so that SOUL will wonder (for the start of
knowing is wonder) "what is it to be
just," "and the end of my meanness," "what is

god like," so that SOUL will know god in the
end, so that, in the last days, SOUL will say
"you are my god" to the right god, not to
some thin likeness of god (maybe the god

will say to me "was she your god" or else
"was the word 'you' your god," for the word of
god is not another to the right-thinking
soul); so that WILL ("the" WILL) will desire heaven,

and WILL will say "earth is just a toy if
god is elsewhere"—we say that anything
we require to complete this purpose is
more or less "good," if not for everybody,

then good for us, and that anything else
is not so good (for you don't know what it
can do to you) or bad. But this "good-for-
you" way of thinking is not good for us.

Disaster: he left a mess.

Music: why don't you just say you were wrong?

Too much beauty: conceal beauty.

Too much talking: no pleasure in talking.

Too much shit: change to shame.

Incomplete word: conceal hole in word.

A BUSINESS IDEA

I'll start a business!
(And I won't let you in it, maybe . . .)

"Let's start a business!"
(in a voice that sounded like money)

"Let's do it!" "We'll start
a business, my brother and me. We'll

invent a machine
to can laughter, and anybody

can have our laughter
for two dollars a can." "You think your

laughter is your own,
to do with as you wish; you think you

can keep your laughter
in a can where it will last, if not

forever, longer
than you will, anyway; you think you

can can it and change
it for money (not much, however).

Maybe someday when
you're down, and you think the sound of it

would heal you, you'll wish
you had your laughter, but all you'll have

is the money." "Mind

your own business." "I'm in the money

business." "That's a good

business." "There's no other business."

GOD IS NOT CAST DOWN

"If we know, we will do, and
we will do the bad thing

you do." You say that in a
knowing voice. But you don't know.

I wish to change everything in my
mind. I wish to change everything.

I do think that something else is
possible for me now, but maybe

not today (seigneur, let there be change).
"There will be change; you don't

have to 'let' it. God is not
cast down; god is a business idea."

ASSHOLE, DICKHEAD, SHIT-FOR-BRAINS

Dear, if you change, I'm left without a choice;
Change, if you doubt, for me there is no doubt;
Doubt, if you're wrong, I'll think all thinking mindless;
Wrong, if you wish, I'll wish myself in two.
        Dear asshole, wise moron, don't toy with me:
Wish, wish

Earth up to heaven, heaven down to hell;
Hell a body of shameless pleasure,
And hell is everywhere. Narrow eyes change
To wide: idea change to fact; fact change
        To word; word "change" change word to thing. So sure,

king, you don't know, you don't
remember

of, a thing, anything
heaven, about me, I say

something
else do, what you, else see

and there's nobody, like I'm, as they
who can talk, talking, don't know how

to you, right now, to talk
to you, ever

like I do, if you ever change
and if you, your mind, begin laughter

WHAT OTHER EYES DO YOU HAVE FOR ME?

talking as we are — now
our desire is — to keep
talking why — would our talking

ever — end naturally — by itself
why would — we ever wish
to — end it if after —

talking to me you — know
nothing about — me what would
that say — about you not

wish — ing to say any —
thing about myself — I'm sorry
for what — I remember I'm —

sorry for what I — don't
remember it — had to be
that way — they may have

been in — my head they
may not — have been I
don't know — just let me

say I'm — sorry for what
I'm — doing right you are —
if you think you are

THIS IS ABOUT AN IDEA I HAD ONCE,
AND I THINK YOU'LL LIKE IT.

I don't know
anything
that

I don't wish to know

anything
else
I cast

out of my mind
I cast you

out of my mind
I cast my mind

out of my body

this is
not what

I think
this is

just something
I've been THINKING

Music: "Why can't I be you"
Music: "To whom were you just now talking"

saying it, desire it, desire it,
you, once, your
no longer, you say you, desire is

at, an end
now talking, must end
mind up, mind up, mind up

everything, system, system
you say is, kind of, everything
a kind of, like a, you say is

a god, the day is
kind of, a god
like, a god

more money, for a business, this is what
suppose, would that, god would do
what if, change, if he had money
god is, anything, inventing

concealing, it's a boy, everything
nothing, without, your eyes
hear me, a, on my throat
I have no, dick, now can you

other voice, it's a boy, hear me
left, not a, choice

| how | a | say | self | can | word |
| can | word | it | how | a | hear |

| it | talk | how | you | me | you |
| self | ing | can | hear | if | have |

| no | to | with | you | hear | a |
| thing | hear | (if | keep | ing | word |

| you | it | mean | thing | sure | a |
| know | must | some | you're | there's | mean |

| ing | where) | do | mean | that | thing |
| some | what | I | by | what | was |

I	ing	bout	don't	my	do
talk	a	I	know	self	you

know	self	kind	voice	you	I
your	what	of	do	have	have

no	of	no	that	know	the
kind	voice	kind	I	of	voice

of	rats	the	of	and	word
the	is	voice	god	here's	200

THE SORE THROAT

"Do you always have to conceal something," he demanded.
"It's as if I'm talking," he remembered.
"For talking I require a voice," he demanded.
"For a voice I require money," he demanded.

"How much money," she demanded.
"Two dollars and some change," he demanded.
He was weeping. "What are you thinking," she demanded.
"How do you know I'm thinking," he demanded.

"For thinking I require a mind," he complained.
"For a mind I require brains," he remembered.
"For brains I require a head," he sighed.
"Guess what's in my mind," he demanded.

"Why is it so difficult for you to remember what's in your own mind," she complained.

"Is this a system," he wondered.

"It's not a business," she gasped.

"The sound of your own voice would disgust you," he complained.

"I'm sure I don't know what you mean," she complained.

"Don't be so sure," he demanded.

"How do you conceal an idea," he wondered.

"My god, my god, I know not what," he remembered.

"Can you hear what I hear," she demanded.

"You don't like anything I do," she complained.

"You don't like seeing me like this," she guessed.

"Keep your eyes on heaven," she demanded.

"Always think about heaven," she demanded.

"Everything you say is impossible," he complained.

"Keep your eyes on god," she was about to say (but he would not let her complete her idea).

"You don't know a thing about money," he complained.

"I don't conceal the fact that I'm bad with money," she sighed.

"How much money do you have in your business," he demanded.

"More than a thousand dollars," she reported.

"That's not so much," he sighed.

"How do you ever know what to say," he demanded.

"I know what I mean, but I can't say it," he gasped.

"Don't you know what I mean," he demanded.

"Is my voice loud," he demanded.

"Like god," she complained.

"It was always there, our business," she remembered.

"It will be there forever," she guessed.

"Are you the word of god," she demanded.

"If I were god I'd be sorry," he gasped.

"It's a good day for seeing a video," she demanded.

"A good day for talking to a moron," she sighed.

"Something in your throat would like to have a word with you," he reported.

"The sore throat is talking to you," he started to say.

"How much longer do I have to have this sore throat anyway," she demanded.

"The god of the sore throat is not a just god," she complained.

"There's a video of myself in your eyes," he reported.

"You do something to me," he gasped.//
"We don't always like the rats who like us," she sighed.//
"I'm your toy," he complained.//
"You mess with my mind," he demanded.

"What purpose are you concealing," he demanded.//
"No wonder you're the way you are," she was saying.//
"I can't change you," she was saying.//
"That's just what you are," she was saying.

"I no longer say what I wish," he complained.//
"I like the way you talk," she demanded.//
"Can you doubt it," she demanded.//
"If there's ever anything I can do for you, anything at all, just let me know," she demanded.

were you, to me, such a, would I
a good, was I, good, remember it
brother, ever, brother, if I was

nothing, your beauty is, in your idea
let down your money, a kind of money, no longer
see heaven, my two eyes, the hem of
your idea, for your idea, can't keep it in
the crust of, your idea
your money seems, more than you, more than
to like me, I mean, you like me

"Do you know what I'm doing to your money," he
      demanded.
"Do you have any idea," he wondered.

can see, in my, me a, say that you think
nothing, head you, gain you, it's all you see
but you won't see, must not, right if I won't
begin, we can't, no rats, left
seeing, begin report, left

keep, where is, keep, that's
everything,
anything, not
in your mind, my mind, in my mind, an idea

money, a, it, a
is a word, kind of, contains, word is a
a word is, money, the other, machine for

reinventing, its, talk, the
itself, other, again, self and
out of, (must we, about, another)

remember, music, how can I, idea

you can have, not my kind, a thing and
it it's not, of thing if, I can have
for me it's, you can have, it too then

there is no, your in, horrible
such thing (if, your own throat, if you can
you can have, what) do you, say a word

and I can, such word (what, saying it) some
say it too, do you do, thing you dislike
there is no, to it by, yourself for doing

THE SORE THROAT

Can't we just talk?

—No.

Talk isn't ever
"just talk." It always
has to be about
something, don't you think?

LET MY BROTHER HEAR MUSIC

who is the owner of this
business it seems to me
we are too brilliant

the sore throat has left
some pleasure

rats dance in a brilliant ring
about your head
how can I be sure
you are not thinking of me

if talking is desire then
all talking is desire and
not just your way of talking

eyes don't ever change

her eyes are weeping
it's her soul that is weeping
it is not my fault

IT IS NO LONGER WE WHO WISH IT

I'm sorry for everything
I'm sorry for everything

that is my fault
I'm sorry for everything

that is not my fault
I'm sorry

about the ring
we won't ever see it again

and we won't ever see another
all I own for that ring

if you
don't like it

don't say it
don't think it

it is not my fault
you must not be sorry

about the ing
I'll invent another

just like it
it is not my fault

and my body change to earth
inventing everything

concealing nothing
it is not that

I'd like to be elsewhere
you say

I'm sorry to hear you say so
I'm sorry for you

you're so downcast
it is not my fault

you can't see heaven
I don't know about god

but I know what I like
you say

I'm not sorry
I'm sorry to hear you say so

I hear your voice as if it were my own

KNOWLEDGE BLOBS

A DOSSIER

The title is an image from William James's psychology. James uses it to describe how memory works: the more you know about a subject, he says, the easier it becomes to recall a particular fact about it, because the facts cling to other facts in a "blob." We use the term here to designate some related procedures: 1) head-and-hand combinations (or nervous habits), particularly 2) binary hand-alphabets, 3) gestural transcriptions from consciously or unconsciously apprehended ambient language into binary hand-alphabets, 4) documentary transcriptions from binary hand-alphabets, 5) translations of previously-existing texts into vocabularies derived from hand-alphabet exercises, as well as 6) clichés, 7) sententia, and 8) documentary accounts of these procedures such as those we present here.

His friend had invented what she called a binary hand-alphabet. After dinner she made the following announcement: "I have invented a binary hand-alphabet . . . 'binary' because a finger is either on or off the table." On the table where they had eaten dinner she demonstrated the insect-like figure of the "s," which, she told him, is called the most harmonious of letters by Joshua Reynolds in his *Discourses on Art*.

It was wrong to say that the fingers represented letters. She had invented an alphabet of gestures, not fingers; not a digital alphabet, a manual alphabet . . . so that a letter was a way of placing the hand. The hand would be placed against some surface, such as a table or another hand. The hand would be poised over the table, and a finger or several fingers would strike the table and remain there before lifting and regrouping. The position of the hand when it struck the table determined what letter it was.

Now she slams her hand against the table, presses it down insistently, as though playing a chord on a keyboard instrument, vamping, holding it down, arpeggiating it to demonstrate the fingering, to show what notes it's made of.

"You seem to be fidgeting."

"I have invented a binary hand-alphabet..."

"You have invented an alphabet of fidgeting."

The relation between the characters isn't specified—they could be, for example, boyfriend and girlfriend, brother and sister, son and mother, doctor and patient or the reverse, student and teacher or the reverse, etc.

She envisions the hand-alphabet as a secret that she and her friend could share. Her friend, however, shows no interest. She then turns her hand-alphabet into a secret that excludes him by teaching it to another friend. Now he starts to get interested. He imagines that everyone around him is sending messages he can't intercept. Calculated to disturb him, their smiles disturb him. Unable to read the hand-alphabet, he imagines that every gesture is part of a language.

"A friend of mine invented a binary hand-alphabet. It looks like this. This is A. This is B. This is C . . . The idea was that she and her friends would be able to talk to one another without anyone else understanding; it would look like fidgeting. I wasn't very interested in it, but I had this kind of paranoid fantasy . . . my friends would be sending messages to one another that I wouldn't be able to read."

Her hands fascinated him. He thought about them constantly. When she put her hand on his shoulder, or approached him from behind and put her arms around him so that her hands met and interlocked in front of him, was she pressing words into his shoulder, his chest, the back of his hand? Could she be communicating something to a person across the room whom (he believed) she knew slightly? Was there a complicated verbal message encoded in a gesture that he could perceive only as a display of companionship and affection (not, admittedly, an uncomplicated gesture, possibly suspect in any case)?

"Am I obsessed with her hands." It was not in his nature to be jealous. This much was evident from his habitual failure to remember the word "jealousy"—for instance, in a conversation about the seven deadly sins.

"The canto in Book II of *The Faerie Queene* where Hellenore's husband becomes, uh . . ." "Jealousy?" "The only instance in the poem of a character actually losing substance and becoming an allegorical figure." "The idea that certain emotions make you less human, less interesting, or simply less complex: you become a type."

It seemed to say something good about him that he couldn't get himself to say the word "jealousy"; someone might say that he didn't know its meaning. But someone else might say that jealousy was so much a part of him that he didn't think of it as something to be ashamed of and couldn't remember that, according to a certain way of thinking, it was a sin.

Now he was jealous of a skill that she had in her hands. It was not a practical skill—as far as he knew it was not—but it created a distance between them in which, it seemed, jealousy was possible. For example, it was possible to be jealous of her friendship with anyone who also knew the hand-alphabet. He tried to think of reasons for not seeing these people, or, at least, not seeing more than one of them at a time; reasons that would not make him feel childish and petty for stating them.

Stage two. Having at last taught himself the hand-alphabet, he now knows that it's practically unreadable; he had not been excluded from anything. Unfortunately he has already internalized the practice of forming words in the hand-alphabet to such an extent that he now compulsively transcribes on his fingers everything he says, hears, reads, or thinks.

"At this point I discovered that it wasn't exactly useful as a means of communication because no one could read it. But I internalized it and started compulsively transcribing conversations . . . I do it with my right hand, though actually I'm left-handed. At first I did it like this, then for a while I did it like this, now I do it like this."

"When you do it like this, are your fingers hitting one another, or is one hand active and the other passive?"

"The left hand is passive; to tell you the truth I don't even know the fingering in my left hand."

For practice, he transcribed "Hugh Selwyn Mauberley" (also called "Life and Contacts") by Ezra Pound. This poem had been written out of a pact made between Pound and T. S. Eliot in which they agreed to write poems in quatrains so that their poems would not be mistaken for Victorian poetry or the works of Amy Lowell. For Pound, it was mainly an exercise, an exercise in frustration . . .

He started with the alphabet, and the poem (a "conversation poem"). Later he transcribed whatever they were saying; or, if there was no one around, whatever he was reading; or, failing that, thinking, if thinking was something that was made of words. Strangely, this practice did not improve his ability to recollect conversations, books, and ideas . . . nor did it encourage him to participate in the conversations.

He had introduced one or two innovations into the system. Instead of using a figure in which all five fingers were in the "on" position to insert a space between words, he knocked on the table with his fist. Then he stopped using the table as a surface to write against, and pretty soon he stopped making spaces. Later he hit on the procedure of using the fingers of the opposite hand in place of the table. Still later he learned to use the tip of his thumb, which was less ostentatious, as a surface; it reduced the scope of the gestures.

Vowels were gradually disappearing from the words. This seemed to be part of the logic of the system, this tendency to disappear. Comment: perhaps all writing and talking would tend to become much faster, blur, and disappear if we didn't have to make ourselves accessible to others. We learn to think very slowly so that others can follow us (using an abnormal use of language as a model for describing a normal one).

At this point he makes the surprising discovery that his hand is still transcribing phrases when he isn't reading or overhearing any conversations and isn't even thinking anything that he's aware of. He becomes especially interested in these phrases and imagines that they are messages from somewhere else or from a more basic part of himself. Having absorbed all his nervous habits, the hand-alphabet now absorbs his conscious existence as well, so that he pays more attention to what his hand is doing than to what's happening around him.

"I was continuing to produce phrases with this hand when there weren't any phrases to transcribe . . . no one was saying anything, I wasn't saying anything, I wasn't thinking anything that I was aware of. It was like a kind of automatic writing, a direct connection between my unconscious and my hand, so that the phrases seemed to come directly from my hand.

"I sort of had to catch myself doing it. I would notice, when nothing was going on and I wasn't thinking anything really, that my hand would get stuck on a certain phrase and repeat it over and over. These phrases, which I thought of as 'white noise' phrases (because they seemed to indicate that nothing was happening in my mind), tended to be somewhat melancholy, for example, 'we have no choice, we have no choice,' repeated over and over."

"Are you getting this down," with a glance at his hands. He knew that he must look nervous, but that, after all, was what a nervous habit was for. He thought that he must look like a ghoul, twitching and tapping his fingers. Or like a person trying to warm his fingers.

"Cut it out, it's driving me crazy."

"That's funny, I would go crazy without it."

Here is my understanding of the project so far. The

project, as I see it, occurs in two distinct stages. In both stages, the hand-alphabet is initially supposed to connect the two characters, but ultimately acts as a barrier. Still, I don't see this as a history of failed communication (which would require that the characters make attempts to communicate, that they have a message to communicate to one another; instead they have a tendency to see messages where there may not be any). Communication remains a paranoid fantasy: "I think that others are communicating." A history of nervous habits: the hand-alphabet is conceived as a medium of communication that merely resembles a nervous habit, and later achieves its destiny by becoming a nervous habit.

"At that time the hand-alphabet absorbed and replaced my other nervous habits, which I didn't particularly mind. The hand-alphabet seemed less embarrassing, less destructive than some of the others."

History of nervous habits. He twists his hair; he eats paper (at a program of avant-garde films he eats the entire program). He puts his mouth against his hand, to wet it, brushing his lips against the little hairs on his wrist . . . is he cleaning himself, like a cat? Is he licking his knuckles? His fingertips?

He covered the back of his head with his hand, as though to prevent the thoughts from escaping. He put the other hand in his book and drew it back and forth, massaging the pages, as though you could get some idea of the contents of a book like that—with one hand in your book and the other on your head.

Family history. His mother picked at her cuticles until they bled. His grandfather had a habit of tracing shorthand symbols in the arm of his armchair. His father smoked. He did not smoke, but he saw something that appealed to him in the paraphernalia of smoking. Selecting a cigarette, placing it between the lips, lighting it with a lighter or with matches, holding it, even simply acquiring the packs of cigarettes and keeping track of them, how many you had and how many you were going to need, gave you something to do with your hands that also involved the mouth.

"I sometimes think that you must play piano, because your fingers are always moving."

"For a long time I brushed my teeth a lot, I mean more than other people do." In fact he was brushing his teeth all the time . . . walking from place to place . . . sitting at his desk he would suddenly get a craving, he would absently take the toothbrush down from the shelf, and since it's still in his hand he might as well do it again. ("Might as well": dangerous expression.) He usually finished by sucking on the bristles of the toothbrush and swallowing the toothpaste (although he did not always use toothpaste), unless he happened to be standing at a sink, in which case he spat it into the sink.

What was strange about it was that he didn't see anything especially strange about it. He must have known that it was considered slightly dangerous to eat toothpaste in these amounts. When his dentist pointed out that his gums were receding slightly, he casually lied about how often and how strenuously he was brushing his teeth. All nervous habits had a destructive element in them anyway . . . if not destructive to the teeth, the fingers, or the scalp, nonetheless destructive to the personality.

It should be emphasized that he had no reason for brushing his teeth (which is forbidden in the bathrooms at train stations: he pretended that the sign had escaped his notice) as often as he did. He was not concerned with the health of his teeth or gums, or their appearance. He did not invent fantasies of dispelling contamination with his toothbrush. He sometimes explained that he liked it, that it gave him a kind of pleasure; that wasn't it. It was a habit he had fallen into and now depended on. Now, wherever he went, he was carrying a toothbrush in the front pocket of his shirt. The head of the toothbrush left a wet spot on his shirtfront; when the wet spot dried, it left a faint white stain, a residue of toothpaste.

He did not know how to respond when people he hardly knew pointed out that he was carrying a toothbrush in his breast pocket.

"Is that a toothbrush in your pocket?"

"Maybe I'm just happy to see you?" As though he had put it there inadvertently.

"It helps me to think; I'm thinking." And if you asked what he was thinking he would say that he didn't know. So why bother to ask? . . . How obvious it was that nothing was going on in his mind as he twisted the hair behind his ear into knots, untwisted the knots and twisted them up again, until the hair behind his ear turned brittle and frail, and the knots came off in his fingers and became nothing. Thus, the real meaning of the gesture: that he was not thinking of anything.

It seemed to him that nothing was going on in his mind a lot of the time. A more likely explanation was that things were going on that he wasn't aware of, things that he could recover only with difficulty.

Comment: what he did to help him think actually prevented him from thinking.

Stage three. At a party he is introduced to a woman who says that she is making a documentary film about his nervous habits. This doesn't surprise him because he has often imagined his life as a film.

"There's someone you should meet." "Hi, what's your name?" "She's making a documentary film." "Yes, I was hoping you would be here, I'm making a film about your nervous habits." "That could be a pretty long film!" "Did you want to ask permission?" "Oh, do I have to ask permission to shoot in his apartment? I promise, you won't even know I'm there?" "Oh, it's not a problem, I'm happy to do it." "What does he mean when he says he's happy to do it? Is he really happy?" "Do you mean to say you're happy?" "Well . . . not 'happy.'"

Scene from a film. "What's the meaning of this gesture?" "It helps me to think; I'm thinking." "What are you thinking?" Trying to think of something he could plausibly be thinking . . . Again: "What are you thinking?" "That question always makes a hash of what I'm thinking." "What are you thinking?" "Why do you ask me to repeat?" "I'm looking for inconsistencies in your story: what are you thinking?" "Do you ask that question only because you already know what I'm thinking? Because what I'm thinking is so obvious?

Or just because it's obvious that I'm thinking something?" "Something in the way you withdraw asks to be drawn out."

A respectful phone call from the documentary filmmaker. Then a disrespectful letter. All the rudeness that she tried to keep out of the phone call is present in the letter. Another letter follows, apologizing for the tone of the previous one but deliberately introducing even greater offenses.

Comment: the function of an apology is to reintroduce the offence in a concentrated form. Or else the apology is directed toward the future: something you're planning (why else would you be so apologetic? "You're not apologizing for what you did; you're apologizing for what you're about to do!").

Fence Books has a mission to redefine the terms of accessibility by publishing challenging writing distinguished by idiosyncrasy and intelligence rather than by allegiance with camps, schools, or cliques. It is part of our press's mission to support writers who might otherwise have difficulty being recognized because their work doesn't answer to either the mainstream or to recognizable modes of experimentation.

The Motherwell Prize is an annual series that offers publication of a first or second book of poems by a woman, as well as a one thousand dollar cash prize.

Our second prize series is the Fence Modern Poets Series. This contest is open to poets of any gender and at any stage of career, and offers a one thousand dollar cash prize in addition to book publication.

For more information about either prize, visit www.fenceportal.org, or send a SASE to:

Fence Books / [Name of Prize]
Science Library 320
University at Albany
1400 Washington Avenue
Albany, NY 12222

For more about *Fence*, visit www.fenceportal.org.

THE MOTHERWELL PRIZE

Living Must Bury — Josie Sigler
Aim Straight at the Fountain and Press Vaporize — Elizabeth Marie Young
Unspoiled Air — Kaisa Ullsvik Miller

THE ALBERTA PRIZE

The Cow — Ariana Reines
Practice, Restraint — Laura Sims
A Magic Book — Sasha Steensen
Sky Girl — Rosemary Griggs
The Real Moon of Poetry and Other Poems — Tina Brown Celona
Zirconia — Chelsey Minnis

FENCE MODERN POETS SERIES

Duties of an English Foreign Secretary — Macgregor Card
Star in the Eye — James Shea
Structure of the Embryonic Rat Brain — Christopher Janke
The Stupefying Flashbulbs — Daniel Brenner
Povel — Geraldine Kim
The Opening Question — Prageeta Sharma
Apprehend — Elizabeth Robinson
The Red Bird — Joyelle McSweeney

NATIONAL POETRY SERIES

The Black Automaton — Douglas Kearney
Collapsible Poetics Theater — Rodrigo Toscano

ANTHOLOGIES & CRITICAL WORKS

Not for Mothers Only: Contemporary Poets on Child-Getting & Child-Rearing
Catherine Wagner and Rebecca Wolff, editors

A Best of Fence: The First Nine Years, Volumes 1 & 2
Rebecca Wolff and Fence Editors, editors

POETRY

Dead Ahead	Ben Doller
My New Job	Catherine Wagner
Stranger	Laura Sims
The Method	Sasha Steensen
The Orphan & Its Relations	Elizabeth Robinson
Site Acquisition	Brian Young
Rogue Hemlocks	Carl Martin
19 Names for Our Band	Jibade-Khalil Huffman
Infamous Landscapes	Prageeta Sharma
Bad Bad	Chelsey Minnis
Snip Snip!	Tina Brown Celona
Yes, Master	Michael Earl Craig
Swallows	Martin Corless-Smith
Folding Ruler Star	Aaron Kunin
The Commandrine & Other Poems	Joyelle McSweeney
Macular Hole	Catherine Wagner
Nota	Martin Corless-Smith
Father of Noise	Anthony McCann
Can You Relax in My House	Michael Earl Craig
Miss America	Catherine Wagner

FICTION

Flet: A Novel	Joyelle McSweeney
The Mandarin	Aaron Kunin

FB